# FOCKE WULF FW 190
## IN ACTION

by JERRY L. CAMPBELL

illustrated by Don Greer

 squadron/signal publications

(Cover) An Fw 190A-8/R7 Rammjäger of IV (Sturm)/JG 3
attacking a stream of B-24's during the fall of 1944.

*To Jillann and Timmy*

ISBN 0-89747-018-4

If you have any photographs of the aircraft, armor, soldiers or
ships of any nation, particularly wartime snapshots, why not share
them with us and help make Squadron/Signal's books all the more
interesting and complete in the future. Any photograph sent to us
will be copied and the original returned. The donor will be fully
credited for any photos used. Please indicate if you wish us not to
return the photos. Please send them to: Squadron/Signal Publica-
tions, Inc., 1115 Crowley Dr., Carrollton, TX 75011-5010.

Photo Credits:
All photographs are from the Bundesarchiv Koblenz
unless otherwise noted. I would like to take this
opportunity to thank Dr. M. Haupt and Herrn Walter for
all of the help they have given.

# Fw 190 Würger

The noted aviation writer, William Green, has pointed out that "it is axiomatic that when a new combat aircraft is added to the inventory, its potential successor should have begun its passage across the drawing boards". Unfortunately for Germany's enemies the potential successor to the Messerschmitt Bf 109, which was reaching first line units, was on the drawing boards of Dipl.-Ing Kurt Tank of the Focke-Wulf Flugzeugbau. Many obstacles, however, would have to be overcome before Kurt Tank's design would be found in the war darkened skies of Europe. Many so-called experts at the Reichluftministerium (RLM-German Air Ministry) felt that the Messerschmitt design was so far advanced that no successor could approach it in performance, and "besides", they were prone to point out, "there was no foreseeable war which would last long enough for another aircraft to find enough employment to justify the expense and time for its development." German military thinking was centered around the concept of a short tactical war.

All breakthroughs in technology and tactics since the First World War led the German military planners to think in terms of short sharp conflicts of movement that would be over in a matter of weeks or at most a few months. The design offered up by Kurt Tank was for an air superiority fighter — a defensive weapon — that according to the prevailing point of view was a totally unnecessary venture. Further, the Focke-Wulf design was based on the bulky radial engine even though it was obvious to the RLM that a low drag liquid cooled engine was essential to the success of a high speed fighter aircraft. However, because Focke-Wulf as yet had no major military contract and because the new design would make no demands upon production of the liquid cooled DB 601 engine which powered the Bf 109, the RLM authorized development of its so-called "second iron in the fire".

During the summer of 1938, under the designation Focke-Wulf Fw 190, the RLM issued a contract for the design and construction of three prototypes to be powered by the BMW 139 eighteen cylinder twin row radial engine. Since Focke-Wulf had surplus drawing capacity, detail design work was begun nearly immediately on the Würger (Butcher Bird) as Kurt Tank had nicknamed it. Because a low priority was attached to the project, the design team, headed by Oberingenieur R. Blaser, was able to proceed slowly and meticulously in order to bring forth an aircraft which "subordinated all details to a single coherent concept . . . offering a greater structural integrity and required a minimum of field maintenance time and could be produced through the use of widely dispersed factories and subcontractors." The resulting prototype was a beautifully proportioned machine that has been described by many as aerodynamically the most beautiful airplane built during World War II. The bulky radial engine was blended into the sleek lines of a fighter aircraft that was a masterpiece of compactness.

During prototype construction it was found that the BMW 139 was not living up to expectations and Bayerische Motoren Werke was anxious to abandon it in favor of the higher rated BMW 801. Although the new engine was almost exactly the same diameter the BMW 801 was somewhat longer and was considerably heavier, causing an extensive redesign of the airframe. The first prototype, the Fw 190V1, was finished with the BMW 139 engine, but the next three prototypes, the V2, V3 and V4, were scrapped in favor of the Fw 190V5 which was powered by the new BMW 801.

The BMW 139 powered Fw 190V1, carrying the code letters D-OPZE, first flew on 1 June 1938 with Focke-Wulf chief test pilot Hans Sander at the controls. Sander described his feelings about the Würger as love at first flight: "I have flown some beautiful aircraft in my time, but I cannot recall one that impressed me more than the delightful Fw 190 from its very first flight". The machine was light on the controls and beautifully balanced with an excellent turning radius (though not to compare with the Spitfire) as well as a quick acceleration and the wide track inward retracting undercarriage was a marked improvement over the notoriously weak landing gear of the Bf 109. The engine was to be cooled by a ten bladed cooling fan, but this was not yet ready for installation when Flugkapitän Sander took the machine on its maiden voyage. The cylinders overheated critically and because of the engines proximity, the cockpit heated to over 130°F and filled with exhaust fumes. Sander later pointed out "since those early flights I had some sympathy for a steak on a gridiron".

Redesigning the fuselage to accept the larger and more powerful BMW 801 engine the Blaser team took this opportunity to solve the host of minor bugs (it was felt that the addition of the cooling fan would solve the overheating problem) that usually accompanied any new design.

The BMW 801 engined Fw 190V5 was completed with a ten bladed cooling fan and a pair of synchronized 7.9mm MG 17 machine guns mounted in the wing roots. Prior to armament trials, the new aircraft was demonstrated to Herman Göring who exclaimed to Kurt Tank that these must be turned out "like hot rolls". Thanks to Göring's enthusiasm, Focke-Wulf shortly received an order for eighteen Fw 190A-0 pre-production machines and one hundred Fw 190A-1 production aircraft.

During the first six months of 1941, a pre-production batch of forty Fw 190A-0s were built and tested carrying an armament of four Rheinmetal Borsig 7.7mm MG 17 machine guns. two mounted in the wing roots and an additional pair mounted in the fuselage just behind the engine; all four were synchronized to fire through the propeller arc. A Revi C/12C reflector gunsight was installed just behind the windscreen above the instrument panel. This quartet of MG 17s did not provide the firepower required by the Luftwaffe and the intention was to install a pair of 20mm Mauser MG 151 cannons in the wing root positions, but this was delayed until synchronization tests could be completed.

By this time, the Luftwaffe had taken severe losses at the hands of the RAF during the Battle of Britain and the air superiority fighter would be needed to guard the Reich's western flank while Germany carried out a "short sharp conflict" against Russia. The war situation had changed to such an extent that AGO at Oschersleben and Arado at Warnemünde were also instructed to begin production of the Fw 190. The air superiority fighter that was to be a second iron in the fire was shortly to be produced by three plants.

The first operational unit to receive the Fw 190 had already been chosen, II/JG 26 "Schlageter", but in order to speed up service

introductions, Erprobungsstaffel 190 was formed at Rechlin-Roggenthin under Otto Behrens and included service personnel from II/JG 26 as well as Focke-Wulf test pilots. The new BMW 801 engine was plagued with teething problems, mainly overheating, and by the time the accelerated test program at Rechlin-Roggenthin was finished, few of these had been solved. Nevertheless on 1 August 1941 testing was transferred to Le Bourget, where the Fw 190 was to be tested under operational conditions by a detachment of II/JG 26 personnel, which was to include mock combat against captured examples of the Spitfire and Hurricane.

This so-called "combat" testing program at Le Bourget quickly degenerated into what has been described as a catastrophe. Engines constantly overheated and cylinders seized up with most take-offs being aborted during run-up. When a take-off was managed, the pilot oftentimes came streaking back to land trailing a stream of black smoke. An investigative commission from the RLM viewing the near chaos recommended that the entire Fw 190 program be cancelled. Fortunately the RLM was persuaded to delay their decision on the future of the new fighter until talks between BMW and Focke-Wulf could be set up to iron out the difficulties. The results of these talks were some 50 modifications and acceptance of the aircraft by the Luftwaffe for serial production.

During the Second World War the BMW 801 powered Fw 190 underwent a number of changes in both equipment and combat role. Through a change of equipment, the Würger was able to perform in the roles of air superiority fighter, fighter-bomber, reconnaissance-fighter, night fighter, bad weather fighter, assault fighter, torpedo fighter and two seated trainer. This was accomplished through a number of Umrüst-Bausätze (factory conversion sets) and Rüstsätze (field conversion sets).

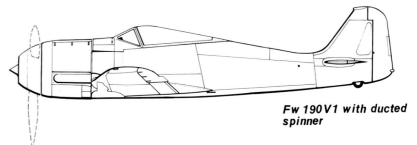

**Fw 190 V1 with ducted spinner**

**The initial prototype, the Fw 190V1, powered by the BMW 139 engine, carried a ducted spinner but since little cooling difference was found the design team opted for the more conventional spinner on subsequent prototypes. (Hans Redemann)**

**Because of constant overheating and subsequent powerplant failure when engine cylinders seized up, the test program at Le Bourget nearly spelled disaster for the fledgling warbird when an RLM commission recommended the cancelling of the entire Fw 190 program. The engine of this aircraft caught fire but the quick acting ground crew put it out with a minimum of damage to the engine.**

5

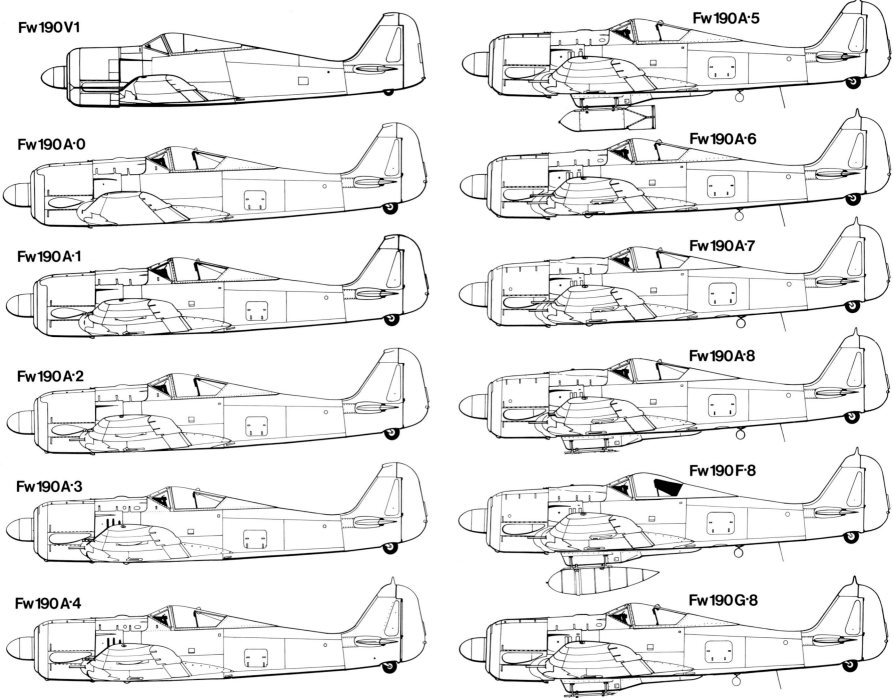

Fw 190 V1

Fw 190 A·0

Fw 190 A·1

Fw 190 A·2

Fw 190 A·3

Fw 190 A·4

Fw 190 A·5

Fw 190 A·6

Fw 190 A·7

Fw 190 A·8

Fw 190 F·8

Fw 190 G·8

# Fw 190A-1

During June 1941 while combat trials were still going on at Le Bourget, the first production Fw 190A-1s began leaving the Focke-Wulf assembly plant at Marienburg. Only minor changes were made to the production Fw 190A-1 in comparison to the preproduction Fw 190A-0 as a result of the accelerated test program at Rechlin-Roggenthin. A cartridge jettison system for the canopy was added since it would not release at speeds above 250 mph. The MG 151 cannons were still not ready so the wing root MG 17s were retained as were the ones in the fuselage, however, in order to increase firepower a pair of 20mm Oerlikon MG FF cannons with 55 r.p.g. were mounted immediately outboard of the undercarriage attachment points. During late July and early August of 1941 the first examples of the Fw 190A-1 were delivered to 6./JG 26, then at Moorseele, Belgium, replacing the Bf 109E-7s and by early September the entire II/JG 26 was equipped with the Würger and III/JG 26 was beginning to trade in their Bf 109Fs for the new mount.

During September the first encounter between the RAF and the Fw 190 took place when four Fw 190A-1s of 6./JG 26 attacked a superior force of Spitfire Vs over Dunkirk. Diving out of the sun the pilots of JG 26 shot down three of the Spits without loss to themselves. The Spitfire V was found to be inferior on every point to the new German fighter with the single exception of turning radius and most importantly the new German fighter's superior speed enabled it to break off combat almost at will. Fortunately for the British the BMW 801 engine was still experiencing teething troubles and most aircraft were usually unserviceable.

A few Fw 190A-1s were sent to the East Front during November of 1941 for service trials with II/JG 54. Trouble with the BMW engine, however, caused its rejection and it would be nearly a year before the Würger would again see service on the Russian Front.

The Fw 190A-1 carried two MG 17 machine guns in the cowling, and one in each wing root, and a 20mm MG FF cannon mounted just outboard of the landing gear. Although not so severe as on the A-0, overheating was still somewhat of a problem as evidenced by the excessive exhaust stains. Halfway between the MG FF and the wing root can be seen the visual undercarriage position indicator, a small finger of metal that raised when the undercarriage was locked in the down position.

A small number of Fw 190A-1s sent to II/JG 54 during November of 1941 for service trials on the Eastern Front. Trouble with the engines coupled with the weather and primitive service condition caused them to be rejected out of hand. (Hans Obert)

# Early Armament Development

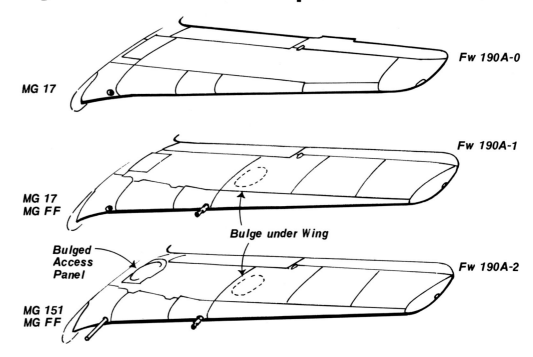

MG 17 — Fw 190A-0

MG 17 / MG FF — Fw 190A-1

Bulge under Wing

Bulged Access Panel

MG 151 / MG FF — Fw 190A-2

Beginning with the BMW 80C-1 engined FW 190A-0 all subsequent models were equipped with a twelve bladed cooling fan. The spiral on the spinner was known as "Spiralschnauze" and was generally painted in the Gruppe color.

(Above Right) Fortunately for the British the Focke-Wulf spent much of its service introduction time with black clad ground crewmen working on the engine. Serviceability remained very low until well into 1942 and had it not been for the highly trained "black ones" the Würger would have seen little action during the first six months of its career.

# Fw 190A·2

By the end of October all 100 examples of the A-1 had been completed and production was terminated in favor of the Fw 190A-2 which had already begun leaving the assembly lines at Warnemünde and Oschersleben. Powered by the improved BMW 801C-2 engine and the wing root mounted MG 17s were replaced by a pair of synchronized 20mm Mauser MG 151 cannons with 200 rounds. The MG 151 installation necessitated the placement of a bulged plate on the inboard upper wing surface. The new engine offered little in added performance but a power boost system, which could be used for one minute, pushed maximum speed to 412 mph at 21,000 ft.

During November 1941 II/JG 26 began receiving the Fw 190A-2, passing their A-1s to the Geschwaderstab. Shortly I/JG 26 received the Fw 190A-2 in the event JG 26 became completely equipped with the new fighter early in the year. The Fw 190As of JG 26 proved their worth during the channel dash of the Gneisenau, Scharnhorst and Prinz Eugen on 12 February 1942. The attacking British lost nearly fifty aircraft of which the Fw 190s bagged the majority, including the total destruction of the Swordfish force sent against the ships.

After more than 400 examples of the Fw 190A-2 were produced, the assembly lines gave way to the Fw 190A-3 during the spring of 1942.

**A ground crewman runs up the engine of Rote Eins (Red One) Werk Number 033 to check for possible roughness while his team mate looks on. This process will be repeated again by the pilot after the ground crew certifies the complaint as being repaired.**

**One serious drawback to the Fw 190 design was the lack of forward vision during taxying and take-off as demonstrated by Red 13. These pilots of 5./JG 26 line-up to check out in their newly received Fw 190A-2s.**

Waiting for the go-ahead this pilot of II/JG 26 will soon be part of a patrol along the coast of France hoping for a shot at intruding Spitfires. The superior performance of the Focke-Wulf was not approached until the Spitfire MK IX made its appearance during the fall of 1942.

# Fw190A·3

During the spring of 1942, the Fw 190A-3 powered by the improved BMW 801D-2 engine was being delivered to JG 26. Producing take-off power of 1700 h.p., the new BMW engine was externally the same with all changes being made internally and the overheating problem was finally solved with the addition of cooling louvers positioned just behind the exhaust outlets. The shape of the symmetrical fairings on the engine cowling were modified in contour. Armament was the same as the A-2.

The Fw 190A-3 was used as a test bed to conduct experiments to explore the feasibility of turning the Würger into fighterbomber and reconnaissance aircraft. After favourable results were obtained, provisions were made on the assembly line to turn out a number of Umrüst-Bausätze (factory conversion sets) equipped aircraft.

**Fw 190A-3/U1** fighterbomber equipped with an ETC 500 bomb rack mounted beneath the fuselage and the MG FF cannon removed.

**Fw 190A-3/U3** fighterbomber was equipped with an ETC 250 fuselage rack and some had additional SC 50 racks on the wing.

**Fw 190A-3/U4** reconnaissance fighter with two Rb 12 cameras mounted in the rear fuselage and the MG FF cannon deleted.

As the Fw 190A-3 became available, the few Fw 190A-1s remaining in service were passed to the fighter schools. The first examples of the new fighter went to JG 26 with JG 2 converting to the Fw 190A-2 and 3 shortly after the "channel dash". A shortage of machines, however, forced III/JG 26 to revert back to the Bf 109F.

Over 500 Fw 190A-3s were produced by the time production was phased out during late 1942 in favor of the Fw 190A-4.

**Receiving the radial engine Focke-Wulf fighter for the first time, the ground crew of this Gruppen is undergoing a familiarization orientation conducted by experienced service personnel. The Fw 190 was designed around the idea of low field maintenance time in order to keep as many aircraft serviceable as possible with a minimum of ground crew. The lower portion of the cowl has already been painted in dark yellow. Yellow nosed aircraft collectively came to be known to Allied airmen as the Abbeville boys.**

**Other than strengthening of the toggle latches and the addition of cooling louvers there were no recognizable external changes made on the Fw 190A-3.**

The Gruppen painter has started to paint out the radio call signs which this A-3 has been delivered with. The call signs were painted out with either a light color or dark color depending on the mood of the painter and what paint was handy. After the radio call signs were overpainted operational markings will be applied. This process goes far to explain some of the more interesting schemes found on the Butcher Bird and many of the variations found in the same unit.

# Cowl Development

Fw 190 A-2            Fw 190 A-3

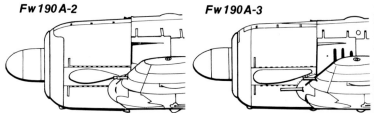

(Above Right) During April 1942 JG 26 began receiving the new Fw 190A-3 relinquishing their A-1s to the Jagdfliegerschule (fighter pilots school).

This aircraft of the same Geschwader has had the factory delivered radio call signs painted out with Dunkelgrün No. 70. The vertical red bar outlined in white indicates it is a machine belonging to III Gruppe almost certainly of JG 26.

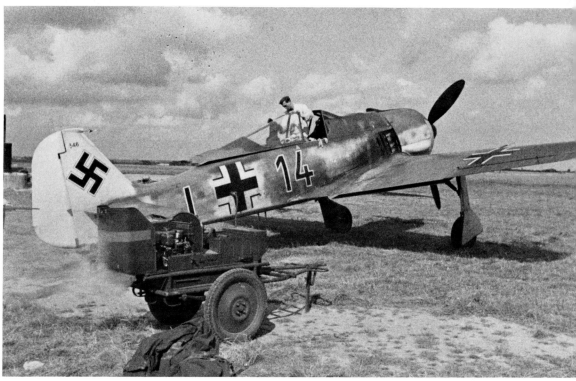

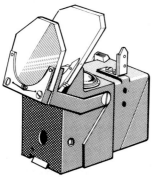

*Revi 16B
Reflector
Gunsight*

(Above) Each Geschwader usually had within its organizational structure an Ergänzungsgruppe (Supplementary Training Unit) to provide advanced training for those replacement pilots just out of training school. This veteran pilot of JG 26 is conducting a training session for these novices of E./JG 26 using a Focke-Wulf model to demonstrate what you do to shake a Spitfire off your tail.

During the middle of the demonstration a flight of Spitfires has been spotted coming in low over the Channel. It is hoped that the tip they received will help keep these novices alive through another mission. Even experience and a superior aircraft however was no guarantee of staying alive when facing experienced British pilots, the first loss of JG 26 after they received the Fw 190 was the Gruppen Kommandeur of II/JG 26 Hauptmann Adolf, a Ritterkreuzträger (Knight's Cross Holder) with 29 kills.

As badly as the Luftwaffe needed the Focke-Wulf fighter during 1942 the German government honored an arms agreement with Turkey by supplying 75 Fw 190A-3s. Operating in mixed units along with Spitfire Vs the Turkish pilots were enthusiastic about the aircraft which remained in service until 1948. (IWM)

(Above Left) During spring of 1942 I and III JG 2 "Richthofen" completely converted from the BF 109F to the Focke-Wulf and II Gruppe had begun. These pilots of 9./JG 2 have moved some "liberated" French furniture onto the flying field so a chess game can be played while they awaited the scramble.

Finding employment in the Mediterranean theater this Fw 190A-3 carries a white spinner tip, panel under the cowling, wing tips, I.D. numbers and fuselage band. After checking the machine thoroughly the ground crew catches up on some reading in the bright morning sun while awaiting the arrival of the pilot.

# FW 190A·3

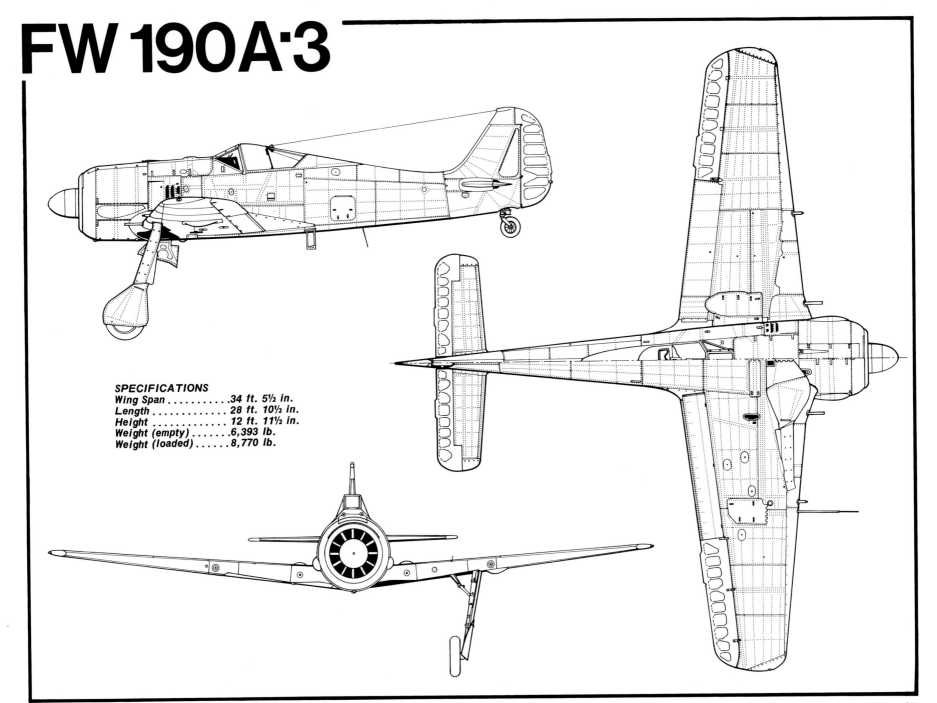

**SPECIFICATIONS**
Wing Span . . . . . . . . . . .34 ft. 5½ in.
Length . . . . . . . . . . . . . 28 ft. 10½ in.
Height . . . . . . . . . . . . . 12 ft. 11½ in.
Weight (empty) . . . . . .6,393 lb.
Weight (loaded) . . . . . .8,770 lb.

# Fw 190A·4

Since most of their bomber force was employed in Russia, the Luftwaffe no longer possessed the strength on the Western Front to carry out normal bombing attacks. It was ordered that each Geschwader based in France was to form a fighterbomber Staffel to carry out low level hit and run raids across the Channel. A 10.(Jabo) Staffel formed initially on Bf 109s were organized within each Geschwader. As the success of these Jabos became more and more apparent, it was decided to equip a number of them with the Fw 190.

To increase its low level performance, the A-4 series was equipped with a Methanol-Water 50 (MW 50) power boost system in order to provide extra power below 16,000 feet. The FuG 7a radio was replaced by a FuG 16z set causing a small vertical pylon to be added to the tip of the vertical fin. To provide additional versatility, a number of Umrüst-Bausätze were instituted.

**Fw 190A-4/U1** Jabo with an ETC 501 bomb rack mounted under each wing with both fuselage and outboard wing armament removed guns being restricted to the wing root MG 151.

**Fw 190A-4/U3** Jabo with an ETC 250 fuselage rack capable of carrying a single 551 lb. SC 250 bomb or a 66 Imp. gal. drop tank. The outboard MG FF cannons were usually removed.

**Fw 190A-4/U8** Jabo-Rei could carry a 66 Imp. gal. drop tank and four 110 lb. SC 50 bombs on wing racks and full armament. With the MG FF cannon removed it could carry two 551 lb. SC 250 bombs on wing racks and a 66 Imp. gal. drop tank, and with both the fuselage MGs and the MG FF cannon removed it could carry a 551 lb. bomb and two 66 Imp. gal. drop tanks beneath the wings. (This Umrüst-Bausatz was a forerunner of the G series.)

During early summer of 1942, the first examples of the Fw 190A-4/U1 went to 10.(Jabo)/JG 26 and a short time later 10.(Jabo)/JG 2 converted to the new type. During the Dieppe raid on 19 August, these two Jabo staffeln took a heavy toll of British landing craft and ships. Throughout 1942 and 1943 these low level attacks against coastal cities tied down large numbers of British fighters and anti-aircraft guns.

**As a result of trials conducted on the A-3 the Fw 190A-4 was designed to accept a variety of bomb racks equipping it as a Jabo (fighter-bomber). This Fw 190A-4/U3 Schlachtflugzeug (assault plane) carries a 1,102 lb. SC 500 bomb on its ETC 500 rack for delivery to the British Isles.**

# Rudder Development

*Fw 190 A-3*

*Fw 190 A-4*

One armorer is holding both MG 151 barrels on the top of the tire, while the other is running the cleaning rod. Although the outboard MG FF cannons have been removed on this aircraft, no bomb racks have been installed. The small inboard undercarriage doors are still on the aircraft.

(Above Left) The first of the new Jabo (fighter-bomber) version of Fw 190A-4 went to a staffel of the veteran Fw 190 Jagdgeschwader 26, 10.(Jabo)/JG 26. The Fw 190A-4/U1 carried a pair of ETC 501 wing racks that could carry a single 551 lb. SC 500 bomb under each wing just outboard of the landing gear. Both MG FF cannons were deleted.

Cleaning and oiling the barrels of the wing root MG 151 cannon was a simple job since they could be removed after rotating them 1/6th of a turn. Every time the barrel was removed, however, the gun had to be readjusted.

The cockpit while well laid out and offering good visibility was not overly roomy and a pilot carrying all the necessary gear for an over-water flight had little room to spare, but certainly more room than found in the Bf 109.

During the fall of 1942 JG 2 received quantities of the Fw 190A-4 until by 10 January 1943 strength reports showed Stab, I and II Gruppen JG 2 were equipped with over one hundred Fw 190A-4s. White 2 of 7./JG 2 is being refueled and rearmed after a sortie.

# Cockpit Interior

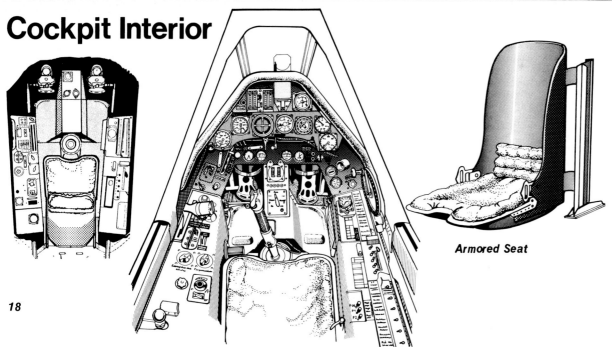

*Armored Seat*

This Ritterkreuzträger of III/JG2 is adding his latest kill to the unit's "victory stick", a practice begun by German pilots during WWI and sporadically continued through WWII.

(Above Left) Carrying an insignia similar to that of III/JG 2 this unknown staffel gets an early morning briefing on an airstrip in France.

The 200 round ammunition storage boxes for the wing root 20mm MG 151s are mounted within the fuselage behind the main wing spar and removed through the wheelwell to be refilled.

During the fall of 1942, I, II and III/JG 51 in turns transferred to Jesau and were re-equipped with the Fw 190A-4, and all three gruppen were back into action before Christmas. Pilots of JG 51 quickly fell in love with the new fighter. One pilot, Lt. Gunther of III Gruppe, who had previously experienced few victories, shot down six Pe 2's on his first sortie with the Fw 190 and by 11 February had run up his score to an impressive thirty. Unfortunately a shortage of Fw 190s forced III/JG 51 to re-equip with Bf 109s.

On this whitewashed machine of I/JG 54 the spinner has been rather lightly sprayed with a white distemper paint, the propeller blades and cooling fan have both caught overspray. Dust stoppers have been slipped over the guns in order to keep blowing snow out of the gun openings.

Carrying both the Geschwader emblem, a green heart below the cockpit, and the Gruppen insignia, shield on the cowling, an Fw 190A-4 of I/JG 54 taxies out to the landing strip to begin a patrol over the snow covered wastes of the Russian forest in the Leningrad area.

During the winter of 1942/43 Stab and II Gruppe JG 54 were equipped with the Butcher Bird flying in mixed units along with Bf 109G in the Leningrad sector under the command of Luftflotte 1.

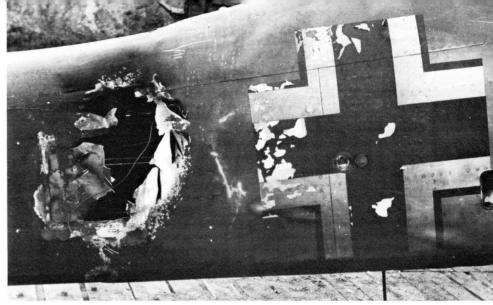

# Undercarriage

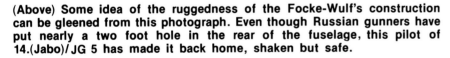

A-3    A-8
MAINWHEEL VARIATION

(Above) Some idea of the ruggedness of the Focke-Wulf's construction can be gleened from this photograph. Even though Russian gunners have put nearly a two foot hole in the rear of the fuselage, this pilot of 14.(Jabo)/JG 5 has made it back home, shaken but safe.

(Above Right) The fuselage structure has been weakened enough that although the pilot made the softest possible landing the spine of the machine nearly broke as evidenced by the wrinkling of the aluminum skinning. The tail wheel retractor cable can be seen hanging free but the rudder and elevator control cables appear to be intact.

Low level fighter bomber attacks against England caught the imagination of the German war correspondents and it has been reported that on at least one occasion a war correspondent was carried in the rear fuselage, the rear access having a plexiglass window inserted. On a number of occasions a downed pilot was picked up by a comrade using this method.

# Fw 190A·5

In April 1943, the Fw 190A-4 began to give way on the assembly line to the Fw 190A-5. Featuring a redesigned and strengthened engine mounting which moved the BMW 801D-2 forward and lengthened the fuselage by 5.9 inches. A small fillet was introduced just in front of the wing root and the fuselage armament cover was increased in length just forward of the forward toggle latch. Other than the above and the fact that the new aircraft was designed to accept a wider variety of Umrüst-Bausätze, the Fw 190A-5 was essentially the same as the A-4. Several Umrüst-Bausätze deserve mention:

**Fw 190A-5/U2** Nacht Jabo-Rei (night long range fighterbomber) equipped with antiglare shields, flame dampners and an ETC 250 fuselage rack and wing racks for a pair of 66 Imp. gal. drop tanks. Armament was restricted to the wing root mounted MG 151s.

**Fw 190A-5/U3** Jabo equipped with racks to enable it to carry up to 2,200 lbs. of bombs and/or drop tanks. Guns were restricted to fuselage mounted MG 17s.

**Fw 190A-5/U4** Reconnaissance fighter equipped with two Rb 12 cameras in the rear fuselage. The MG FF cannons were removed.

**Fw 190A-5/U8** Jabo-Rei was fitted to carry a 551 lb. SC 250 bomb under the fuselage and two 66 Imp. gal. drop tanks mounted under the wing. Armament as with the U2 and U3 was restricted to the wing root MG 151s.

With the increasing strength of 8th Air Force 4-engine bomber raids, German pilots were hard pressed to find a method of attacking the tight formations of bombers that would create the greatest loss to the enemy, and at the same time, minimize losses to themselves. Experienced pilots had worked

**The 5mm armour cowling ring on this Fw 190A-5/U3 has been painted bright yellow while the spinner is black with a white tip.**

**Werk No. 7099, an Fw 190A-5 of 8./JG 2 at Cherbourg during the fall of 1943. Because of a shortage of Fw 190s III/JG 2 operated both Fw 190As and Bf 109Gs until May 1943 when the Gruppe was again equipped entirely with the Würger.**

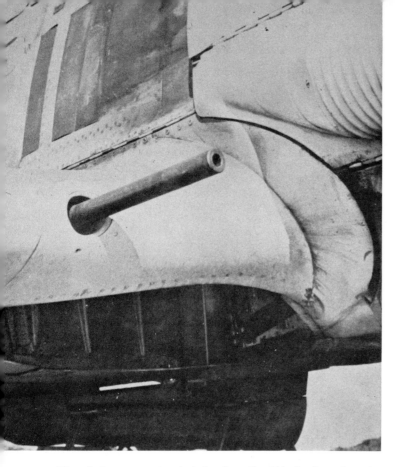

out tactics of a head on attack at the same altitude as the bombers, waiting until the last second to dive under or to pull over the bomber. Many of the younger, less experienced pilots could not judge the closing speed of their aircraft adequately and lost their lives when they crashed into the target. The method of attack was changed, the attack was still made from the front, but at an angle of 10 degrees so a collision was unlikely.

On 14 October, the Fw 190A-5/R6s of JG 1 and JG 26 equipped with Wfr. Gr. 21 mortars fired their projectiles from outside the range of the B-17s defensive gun range and the ensuing explosions broke up the tight defensive formations allowing the Luftwaffe to hunt down and destroy dozens of individual aircraft. The USSAF lost 62 bombers with a similar number damaged to the point of write-off. This raid against Schweinfurt was the most costly Allied raid of WWII.

The A-5 was extended in length 5½ inches by the simple insertion of a fillet just in front of the wing fairing.

(Above Right) Somehow this staffel kommandeur has been able to get his hands on an Fw 190A-5 with which he is leading his staffel of Bf 109s. Because it could absorb a lot of punishment and still fly, the Fw 190 was highly prized by pilots on the Eastern Front.

Knights Cross holder, Josef "Sepp" Wurmheller (left), Staffel Kapitän of 9./JG 2 grabs a cigarette with his wing man after a mission against marauding RAF Spitfires. Wurmheller gained 102 victories (9 on the East Front, 93 on the West Front including at least 13 four engined). On 8 July 1944 he was promoted to Kommandeur of III JG 2 and was killed during a dogfight over France when he collided with his wing man just 14 days later.

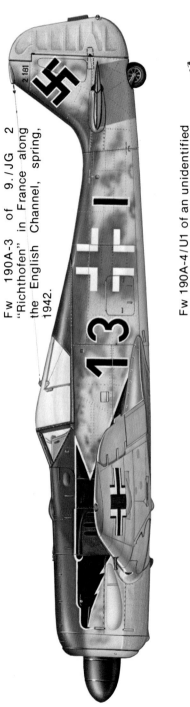

Fw 190A-3 of 9./JG 2 "Richthofen" in France along the English Channel, spring, 1942.

Fw 190A-4/U1 of an unidentified unit in France during the summer of 1943. Quite possibly one of the several autonomous Gruppen operating at this time.

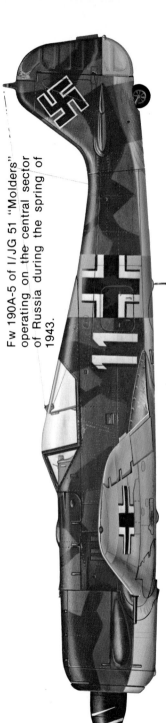

Fw 190A-5 of I/JG 51 "Molders" operating on the central sector of Russia during the spring of 1943.

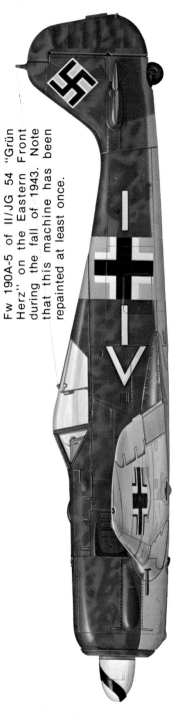

Fw 190A-5 of II/JG 54 "Grün Herz" on the Eastern Front during the fall of 1943. Note that this machine has been repainted at least once.

Fw 190A-6 of I/JG 54 "Grün Herz" believed flown by the Ace Walter Nowotny.

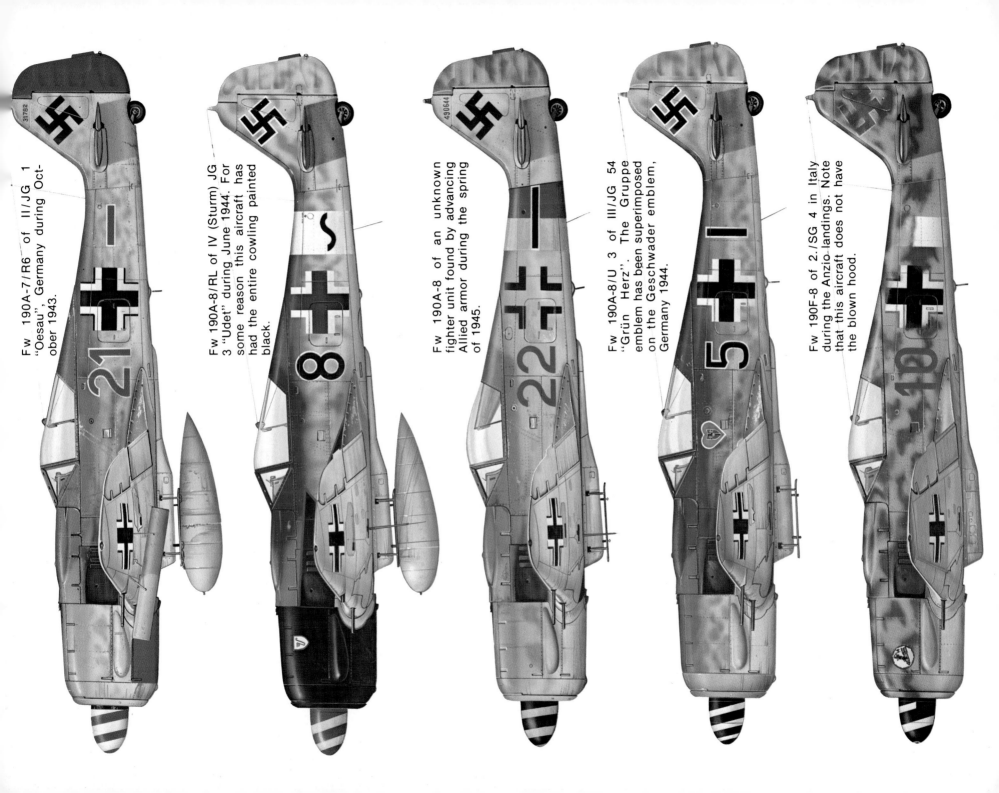

Fw 190A-7/R6 of II/JG 1 "Oesau", Germany during October 1943.

Fw 190A-8/RL of IV (Sturm) JG 3 "Udet" during June 1944. For some reason this aircraft has had the entire cowling painted black.

Fw 190A-8 of an unknown fighter unit found by advancing Allied armor during the spring of 1945.

Fw 190A-8/U 3 of III/JG 54 "Grün Herz". The Gruppe emblem has been superimposed on the Geschwader emblem, Germany 1944.

Fw 190F-8 of 2./SG 4 in Italy during the Anzio landings. Note that this aircraft does not have the blown hood.

# Rüstsätze (Field Conversion Kits)

Several different armament or equipment sets called *Rüstsätze (Field conversion Kits)* could be installed in normal production models. The following chart gives full particulars and shows the aircraft models so equipped:

**R1** Radio set FuG162 for guiding fighters.

*Fw 190A-4/R1, Fw 190A-5/R1*

**R1** One WB151/20 gun pack under each wing.

*Fw 190A-6/R1, Fw 190A-7/R1 Fw 190A-8/R1*

**R2** One Mk108 30mm cannon under each wing.

*Fw 190A-6/R2, Fw 190A-7/R2 Fw 190A-8/R2*

**R3** One Mk103 30mm cannon under each wing.

*Fw 190A-6/R3, Fw 190A-8/R3*

**R4** GM1 power booster (nitrous oxide power boost system).

*Fw 190A-6/R4, Fw 190A-8/R4*

**R5** One 115 ltr. fuel tank in fuselage.

*Fw 190A-8/R5*

**R6** One WGr21 rocket projectile under each wing.

*Fw 190A-4/R6, Fw 190A-5/R6 Fw 190A-6/R6, Fw 190A-7/R6*

**R7** Armor glass for canopy.

**R8** Armor glass and Mk 108 cannon in wing outboard position.

*Fw 190A-8/R8*

**R11** Radio set FuG125, direction finder PKS 12 and heated cabin windows for all weather operation.

*Fw 190A-8/R11*

**R12** Radio set FuG125, direction finder PKS 12, heated cabin windows for all weather operation and one MK108 cannon in each wing.

*Fw 190A-8/R12*

These Fw 190A-5s operating on the Eastern Front during the fall of 1943 belong to II/JG 54. The machine in the foreground carries an extremely interesting scheme that shows signs of being repainted at least once.

# Fuselage Development

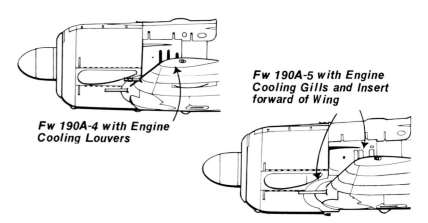

Fw 190A-4 with Engine Cooling Louvers

Fw 190A-5 with Engine Cooling Gills and Insert forward of Wing

(Above Left) Carrying very unusual markings, this Fw 190A-5 fighter bomber belonging to an as yet unidentified unit, taxies from its dispersal area on its way to a fighter bomber mission carrying an SC 500.

White "4", another machine of II/JG 54, also shows signs of being repainted. Also note the replacement access panel.

(Above) Feldwebel Adolf Glunz who survived the war with over 70 kills, most of which were in the Focke-Wulf, is showing a green pilot some techniques he has picked up while using the Revi gunsight to make a deflection shot. (Hans Rossbach)

# Wing Drop Tanks

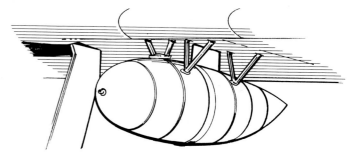

(Above Left) Returning from a sortie this Rotte of A-5s taxies into the densely wooded area surrounding their airfield. Using a heavily wooded area to disperse their aircraft was nearly mandatory after Allied fighters began ranging into northern Germany during early 1944.

This Fw 190A5/U2 although constructed as a nocturnal Jabo Rei prepares for a daylight mission. Because of the acute shortage of aircraft during 1942 and 1943 the Luftwaffe could not afford to use aircraft only for a specialized purpose.

Oberstleutnant Josef "Pips" Priller, the Kommodore of JG 26, arrives in his personal staff car already wearing flying boots and pants.

(Right) Priller's aircraft carried the Ace of Hearts with *Jutta* written on it, on both the port and starboard sides. The top of the Revi gunsight can clearly be seen on the top of the leather padded instrument panel.

Because of heavy Allied bombing just prior to D-Day, JG 26 had been dispersed, I Gruppe going to Metz, II Gruppe to Rheims and III Gruppe to the south of France. When the invasion came only Priller and his wingman, Feldwebel Heinz Wodarczyk, were in a position to get over the beaches. The Luftwaffe on 6 June 1944 were able to put only two aircraft into the air to stem the tide of the Allied onslaught.

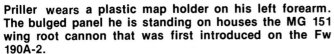

Priller wears a plastic map holder on his left forearm. The bulged panel he is standing on houses the MG 151 wing root cannon that was first introduced on the Fw 190A-2.

(Above Right) The ground crew has just replaced the radio, a minor maintenance task, on the Butcher Bird while the pilot looks like he might need a little help adjusting his parachute harness.

Replacing the rear flying surfaces and tail wheel was a task that could be accomplished at nearly any forward base if the replacement parts were available. Focke-Wulf provided a special sling type of trestle with which to lift the tail clear of the ground, but this was usually not available and other types of trestles, as above, were usually pressed into service. When the rear fuselage was trestled a weight of 157 lbs. had to be added and if the tail unit was removed 386 lbs. had to be added.

# BMW 801

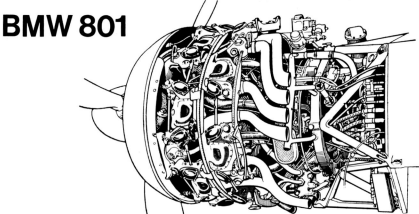

(Above Left) Since the oil cooler was mounted inside the armored cowl just behind the cooling fan it was a simple matter to remove the oil cooler for repairs.

Taking it off or putting it back on was a two or three man job besides the man on top that will guide the mounting holes over the mounting bolts.

(Above) After the oil cooler has been secured into place the various hoses and fittings must be connected, but even this was not overly time consuming.

# Fw 190A·6

By 1943, the variety of roles and consequent increase in equipment caused a weight escalation that became an increasing cause for concern. Focke-Wulf set about redesigning the internal wing structure in order to solve this loading problem. Going into production during June of 1943 under the designation Fw 190A-6 the aircraft was designed primarily for use on the Eastern Front and was capable of accepting a variety of Rüstsätze rather than Umrüst-Bausätze. More heavily armed and armored, the new fighter standardized on a pair of fuselage mounted MG 17s and four wing mounted 20mm MG 151s.

The Rüstsatz normally fitted was the R1 and R6. Arado, AGO and Fiesler built some 569 by the end of 1943. The standard fighter as well as those machines equipped with Rüstsätzen were pressed into service on the Western Front as a Pulk-Zestörer (bomber formation destroyer).

## A·6 Wing Armament

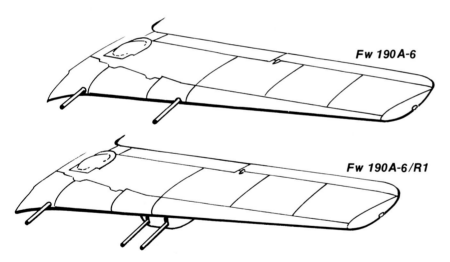

*Fw 190 A-6*

*Fw 190A-6/R1*

The wide track of the Focke-Wulf is seen to advantage on this factory fresh A-6 awaiting delivery to an operational unit. The angle of the landing gear oleos present an appearance of delicateness when in fact it was quite rugged.

The Fw 190A-6 carried the standard two 7.9mm 151 machine guns in the fuselage and four wing mounted 20mm MG 151 cannons. Although the machine was designed for use on the Eastern Front with extra armour provided around the engine and pilot, this machine belongs to 6./JG 26 operating against USAF bomber streams during March 1944.

To ease entry and exit from the cockpit a self-sealing kickplate step was provided midway up the fuselage.

(Above Right) This Fw 190A-6 was equipped with a gun camera which can be seen mounted midway between the two MG 151s.

Gruppen Kommandeur of I/JG 54, Walter Nowotny, believed to be piloting this aircraft, ended the war with 258 kills when he was shot down while flying an Me 262 only weeks before the war ended.

Remanufacturing written off aircraft increased aircraft production tremendously. This hangar full of fuselages awaiting remanufacture was found near Kolleda after the area was overrun by the U.S. 1st Army. (USAF)

# Fw 190A·7

Before the end of 1943, the Fw 190A-7 was put into production and while only some eighty machines were delivered, it was the first aircraft to standardize on the 13mm MG 151 fuselage guns mounted under a new bulged fuselage armament panel just in front of the windscreen, a Revi 16B gunsight being provided. At least half of the machines delivered were Fw 190A-7/R2 Zerstörer mounting a pair of 30mm Mk 108 cannon instead of the outboard MG 151s.

## Armament Development

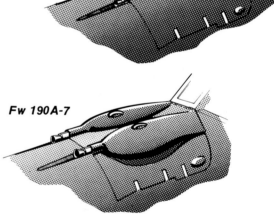

*Fw 190A-6*

*Fw 190A-7*

Only some 80 Fw 190A-7s were produced, and mostly as R2 Zerstörer with 30mm Mk 108 cannons but some were fitted with Wfr.Gr. 21 Mortars under the designation Fw 190A-7/R6 Pulk-Zerstörer.

The rocket tube hangs beneath the outboard weapons bay suspended from a hook which is secured to wing rib 8.

# 13mm MG131 Installation

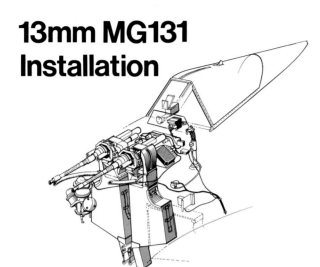

# A·7 Wing Armament

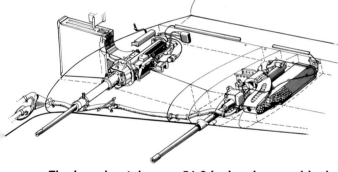

The launcher tube was 51.2 inches long and had three guide rails on the inner surface of the tube. The rocket was fired by depressing the bomb release button on the control column grip.

Initially very successful against the 8th Air Force daylight bomber formations, rocket equipped Fw 190As broke up a 228 aircraft B-17 formation costing the USAAF total losses of nearly 50 percent. By the time A-7/R6 came into production, however, the Luftwaffe had to first fight escorting fighters before attacking the bombers, the loss of aerodynamic qualities when the rocket tube was attached was so great that its use had to be discontinued.

# Fw 190A·8

The last production version of the Focke-Wulf Fw 190A-8 was to be built in larger numbers than any other version with over 1300 machines being produced during the course of 1944. Standardizing on the basic armament of the A-7, the BMW 801D-2 engine was equipped with an MW 50 (Methanol-Water) boost system providing 1700 h.p. for take-off and 1440 h.p. at 18,700 feet. The boost system was provided with a 25 gal. reservoir tank situated behind the pilot's seat with provision for replacement by a fuel cell of equal capacity, to rebalance the center of gravity the ETC 501 bomb rack, when fitted, was moved forward eight inches.

During the spring of 1943, one of the more interesting variants of the A-8 series was the Fw 190A-8/R8 assault fighter used by the so-called Sturmstaffel or Rammjäger. At the suggestion of Major von Kornatski, volunteers from other units formed Sturmstaffel 1 in which each pilot signed a declaration that he would not return without having destroyed an enemy bomber, even to the point of ramming as a last resort. Soon the other Geschwadern began forming Sturmstaffeln of their own. Eventually these were brought together under the special home defense Jagdgeschwader z.b.V. under the command of Maj. Walter Dahl.

(Above Left) With all panels removed the compact mass of the twin row 14 cylinder BMW radial engine is revealed. The intake tube sticking up just between the MG 131s provided fresh air to the cockpit.

Normal armament for the Fw 190A-8 consisted of a pair of MG 131s in the fuselage and four MG 151s in the wings. This machine, an Fw 190A-8/R2 had the outer wing panel MG 151s replaced by a pair of MK 108s. For some reason this Würger belonging to JG 3 has had its entire cowling area painted black; the spinner is red with a yellow spiral.

(Right) The Fw 190A-8/R7 Rammjäger carried additional armor plating around the MK 108 cannons and cockpit and also had special armored glass panels fitted to the canopy sides. The Rammjäger, Jagdgeschwader z.b.V., was formed by drawing five gruppen from various Geschwader of which IV(Sturm)/JG 3 and III(Sturm)/JG 54 were two.

Carrying red and yellow Defense-of-the-Reich tail bands with a black horizontal bar, this Fw 190A-8 belonging to II/JG 301 was abandoned in the face of advancing Allied armor. (Gene Stafford)

*Armor Placement*
*Fw 190A-8/R7*

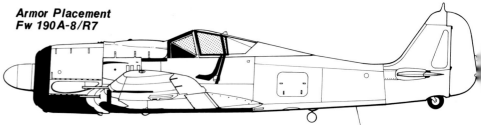

(Above Left) With his Fw 190-A-8/R7 in the background, Major Walter Dahl discusses "Sturm" tactics with other pilots of his Rammjäger. Each pilot signed a declaration that he would not return from a sortie without having destroyed an enemy bomber. The pilots would press their attack close enough that when all else failed they could ram the enemy aircraft, and many did. (Hans Rossbach)

An Fw 190A-8 belonging to JG 1 sits in the background as Luftwaffe ground personnel mine the airfield in preparation for its destruction in the event of Allied threat.

Once turning out Focke-Wulf fighters "like hot rolls" the giant factory at Oschersleben was reduced to the storage and repair of damaged aircraft by the war's end. (USAF)

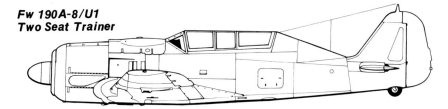

*Fw 190A-8/U1*
*Two Seat Trainer*

(Above Right) Among the aircraft belonging to a training unit can be seen a Fw 190A-8/U1 two seated trainer. Of particular interest is the variety of color schemes found in this line up. (IWM)

The Fw 190s successful use as a night fighter with Wilde Sau units during 1943 led to experimental installation of radar on the single seater. Equipped with FuG 216 radar this Fw 190A-8/R11, bristling with Letzler antennas, was operational during late 1944 with NJG 10.

Under the direction of Albert Speer underground factory complexes were
constructed during 1944. The components were built at diversified
locations and shipped to one of these underground plants for assembly.
In this way the Germans were able to turn out more aircraft than ever
before. (USAF)

# FW 190A·8

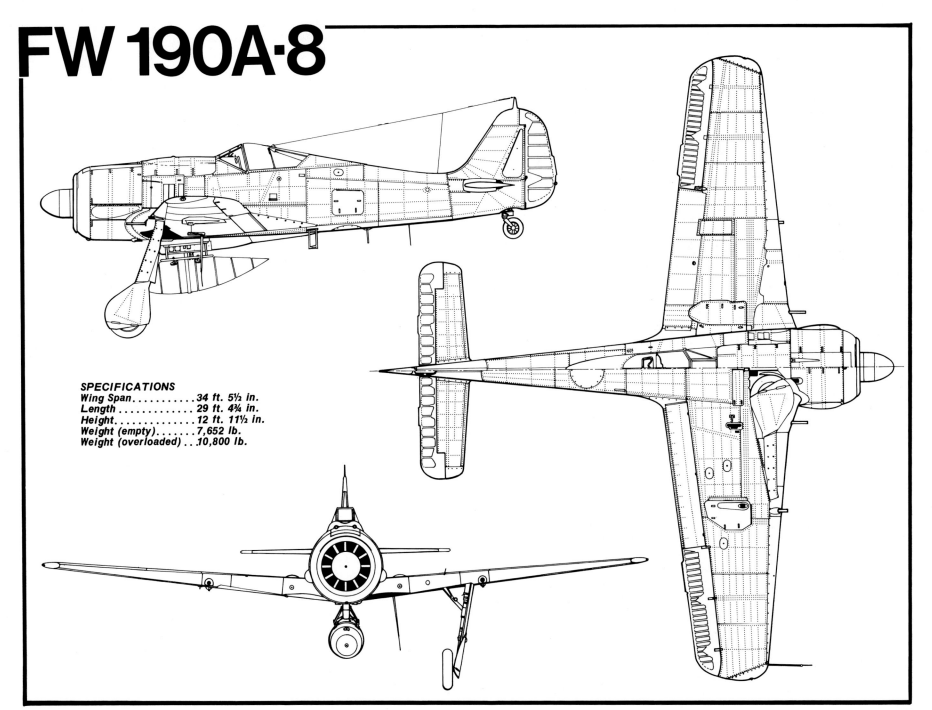

**SPECIFICATIONS**
Wing Span...........34 ft. 5½ in.
Length .............29 ft. 4¾ in.
Height.............12 ft. 11½ in.
Weight (empty).......7,652 lb.
Weight (overloaded) ..10,800 lb.

# Fw 190F

Since the Fw 190 had shown an adaptability to the dive bomber role and because the Ju 87 Stuka was becoming more and more obviously obsolete, it was decided during the fall of 1942 to manufacture a variant designed specifically for the close support role. The series was based on the Umrüst-Bausatz 3 consisting of an ETC 501 rack capable of carrying a 1,102 lb. bomb or an adapter that would allow four 110 lb. SC 50 bombs to be carried and optional wing racks for a pair of 551 lb. SC 250 bombs under each wing. Additional armor protection was added for the pilot; the undercarriage was strengthened and the pitot tube was moved to the starboard wing tip position.

> **Fw 190F-1,** a rather crude assembly line conversion based on the shorter A-4 airframe. Only some thirty examples were built during the second half of 1942.

> **Fw 190F-2** based on the longer A-5 fuselage but otherwise similar to the F-1 this variant featured for the first time a blown hood. A number of these aircraft were tropicalized with sand filters and used in Tunisia and the Mediterranean theater. 271 machine guns were produced between the end of 1942 and the spring of 1943.

> **Fw 190F-3** based on the A5/U17 but had the strengthened wing of the A-6. The ETC 501 rack was replaced with an ETC 250 that would accept an SC 250 bomb or a 66 Imp. gal. drop tank. Built by Arado some 247 aircraft were produced.

After some 550 F series aircraft were built, production was halted in favor of the G series. It was not until the spring of 1944

**The F series was standardized on the Umrüst-Bausatz 3 consisting of an ETC 501 fuselage rack, plus the addition of optional wing racks for carrying a SC 250 bomb under each wing. The first production machine, the Fw 190F-1, was an assembly line conversion using the shorter Fw 190A-4 airframe as a basis. Equipped with Fw 190F-1s, II/SG 2 took crippling losses during the Allied invasion of Sicily while operating from Sardinia. (Smithsonian)**

**This colorful Fw 190F-2 of an unidentified Schlachtgruppe on the Eastern Front carried a yellow fuselage band, yellow wing tips, a yellow cowling ring and a yellow spinner with a black spiral. The code letters are white.**

that Fw 190F production was resumed, now based on the A-8 airframe.

**Fw 190F-8**, as with the A-8, the F-8 carried a pair of 13mm MG 131 machine guns under a bulged hood just behind the engine cowling and carried a repositioned bomb rack. 385 aircraft were built.

**Fw 190F-9** had a BMW 801TS engine offering 2000 h.p. for take-off and emergency.

The wing racks on the Fw 190F-3 were optional and were oftentimes not fitted, since over twenty miles per hour off the top speed was lost when these racks and their loads were carried. These rather unusual markings belong to II/SG 4.

This rotte of Fw 190F-3/R1s from an unknown Schlachtgeschwader lift into the afternoon sunlight, each aircraft carries a single 551 lb. on the belly rack and four SC 50s on the wings. Based on the Fw 190A-6 airframe, the F-3/R6 could mount a pair of 30mm cannons attached outboard of the landing gear replacing the four smaller bomb racks, only some twenty of these aircraft were delivered however.

Due to perhaps a shortage of material, these Fw 190F-8s of I/SG 4 are not equipped with the blown hood.

Based on the Fw 190A-7/8 airframe the Fw 190F-8 featured a pair of MG 131 fuselage machine guns under a bulged cover.

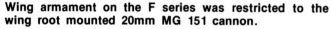
Wing armament on the F series was restricted to the wing root mounted 20mm MG 151 cannon.

(Above Right) Probably delivered in the standard European scheme of 65/70/71, Red 10, an Fw 190F belonging to 2./SG 4, has had the upper surfaces over-painted with 79 Sandgelb and 80 Olivgrün. Of great interest is the over-painting of the swastikas, upper portions of the tail band and wing crosses.

(Right Center) Fighting a losing battle against the Russian juggernaut Sg 2 flew mission after mission strafing enemy columns pushing their way toward Germany. But for each soldier or piece of equipment lost, the Russians seemed to replace their losses with two more. (Hans Obert)

For some reason a V has been painted on both the upper and lower port wing surfaces of this machine of SG 2 during January 1945 in Hungary. (Hans Obert)

Plowing through snow to lead this formation aloft, the Gruppen adjutant of Sg 2 moves onto the runway. The adjutant's Fw 190F-8 has had the wing racks removed but the aircraft behind him, also an F-8, carries bombs on the wing but not a blown hood. (Hans Obert)

*ETC 71 Wing Racks*
*with SC 50 bombs*

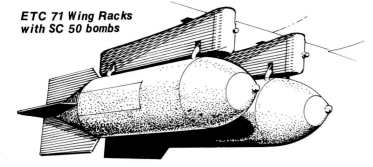

(Above Right) A line up of Fw 190F-8s belonging to 2./SG 2 shows several variations of winter camouflage schemes. The wheel pants have been removed to keep snow and mud from collecting. (Hans Obert)

This Fw 190F-8 belonging to the III Gruppe of an unknown Geschwader took part in "Operation Bodenplatte" in which 700-800 Luftwaffe fighter and fighter bombers made a surprise attack on Allied airfields in France, Belgium and Holland. The attack was marginally successful until the returning aircraft flew over an area infested with flak emplacements protecting V-2 sights. Nearly 200 German aircraft were shot down by German flak. (Hans Obert)

# Fw 190 G

Developed in parallel with the F series was the Fw 190G Jagdbomber mit Vergrösserter Reichweite (Long range fighterbomber) or Jabo Rei, as it was usually called. It was based on the Umrüst-Bausätz 13 as applied to the A-4 and A-5 consisting of a fuselage ETC 501 fuselage bomb rack and wing racks for a pair of 66 Imp. gal. drop tanks. The fuselage MG 17s and outboard MG FFs were removed restricting armament to the wing root MG 151s.

**Fw 190G-1** built by Focke-Wulf, Arado and Fiesler and based on the A-4 airframe, the G-1 had a maximum range of 932 miles. The wing tanks were originally designed for the Ju 87, the machine the G series was replacing. Production was terminated after 49 examples were built.

**Fw 190G-2** was identical to the G-1 except that it was based on the longer A-5 airframe. A total of 468 aircraft were built during 1942-1943.

**Fw 190G-3** going into production during the summer of 1943 carried as standard equipment the PKS 11 directional control and Focke-Wulf designed bomb racks and external tankage, and a robot camera installation was provided.

The **G-4**, **G-5**, **G-6** and **G-7** were projects only.

**Fw 190G-8** was a counterpart of the A-8 and incorporated most of the design modifications found on that model. Compared to the G-3, the following modifications were made: MW 50 fuel injection, which was replaceable by a 25 gallon fuel tank, was standard. ETC 501 fuselage rack moved forward 8 inches (non-jettisonable). Range with a pair of 66 Imp. gal. fuel tanks and one SC 500 bomb was increased to 1,052 miles. Production was terminated in February 1944 and replacement machines were provided by modification of Fw 190F-8s by forward maintenance crews.

Carrying a pair of 66 Imp. gal. drop tanks under the wings, the Fw 190G-1 had a maximum range of 930 miles. When flying across the steppes of Russia this increased range became very important.

The Fw 190G-2 was based on the longer A-5 fuselage and was built in substantial numbers. These brand new G-2s have just been delivered to an unidentified Jabo unit that has painted out the factory call signs but as yet has not added operational markings.

During August of 1943 front line units began receiving the Fw 190G-3 with the improved BMW 801D-2 engine that had a fuel injection system and a boost system that increased maximum loaded speed up to 356 mph.

This staffel operating Fw 190G-3s in concert with BF 109Gs belong to an unidentified Schlachtgeschwader on the Eastern Front during the winter of 1943/44. Interestingly, the port wheel pants have been removed while the starboard ones have been left intact.

Under the designation Fw 190G-8/R5 146 late production aircraft were fitted with four ETC 50 racks mounted under the wing. The aperture outboard of the wing racks is a cine camera.

Expecting a severe snow storm this Fw 190G-8 has been almost completely covered with canvas to keep ice from forming on the flying surfaces.

These colored soldiers of the 4046th Truck Company found the AGO aircraft works at Oschersleben a source of souvenirs. (USAF)